Introduction

This book introduces the structure and function of the human body.

In this module you will learn to:

- Describe basic human body functions and life process.

- Name the major human body systems and relate their functions.

- Describe the anatomical locations, structures and physiological functions of the main components of each major system of the human body.

Need-to-know

Metabolic, having to do with metabolism (the total of all chemical changes that take place in a cell or an organism to produce energy and basic materials needed for important life processes).

Homeostasis, a state of balance among all the body systems needed for the body to survive and function correctly.

The human body is a single structure but it is made up of billions of smaller structures of four major kinds: <u>Cells</u>, <u>tissues</u>, <u>organs</u> and <u>system</u>.

Cells

Cells have long been recognized as the simplest units of living matter that can maintain life and reproduce themselves.

They provide structure for the body, take in nutrients from food, convert those nutrients into energy, and carry out specialized functions.

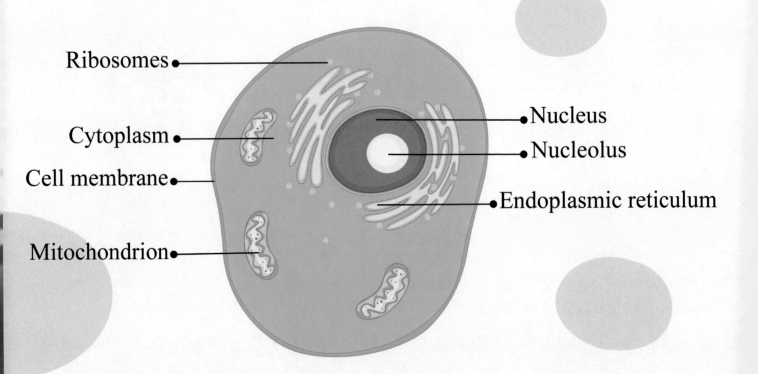

Tissues

By definition, a tissue is an organization of a great many similar cells with varying amounts and kinds of nonliving, intercellular substance between them.

The four types of tissues:

Nervous tissue is responsible for coordinating and controlling many body activities.

Muscle tissue is composed of cells that have the special ability to contract in order to produce movement of body parts.

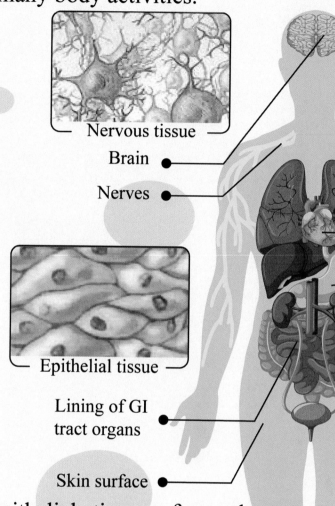

Nervous tissue

Brain

Nerves

Muscle tissue

Skeletal muscle

Cardiac muscle

Smooth muscle

Epithelial tissue

Lining of GI tract organs

Skin surface

Connective tissue

Fat

Bone

Epithelial tissues form the covering of all body surfaces, line body cavities and hollow organs, and are the major tissue in glands.

Connective tissues bind structures together, providing support and protection.

GI tract organs: The organs that food and liquids travel through when they are swallowed, digested, absorbed, and leave the body as feces.

Organs

An organ is an organization of several different kinds of tissues so arranged that together they can perform a special function.

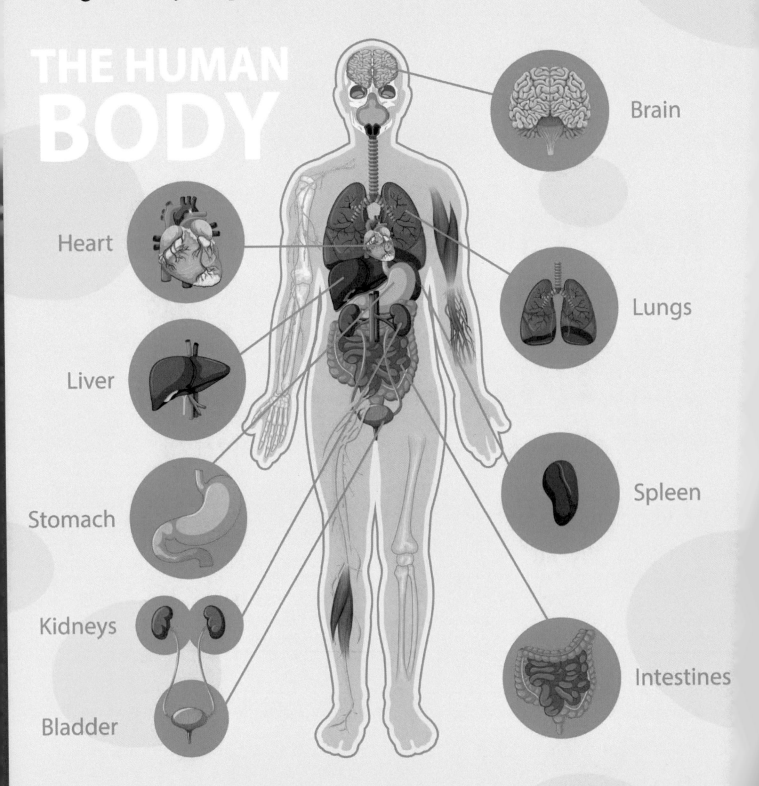

THE HUMAN BODY

Brain

Heart

Lungs

Liver

Stomach

Spleen

Kidneys

Intestines

Bladder

Heart:

The heart is one of the most vital organs. It is on the left side of the body in humans and is about the size of a fist. It pumps blood throughout the body. Its function is vital because, to survive, the tissues need a continuous supply of oxygen and nutrients, and metabolic waste products have to be removed.

The normal adult heart pumps about 5 liters of blood every minute throughout life.

Cardiac and cardio both mean "about the heart", so if something has the prefix cardio or cardiac, it has something to do with the heart.

The human heart has four chambers. Some animals have only two or three chambers.

In humans, the four chambers are two atria and two ventricles. Atria is talking about two chambers; atrium is talking about one chamber. There is a right atrium and right ventricle. These get blood that comes to the heart. They pump this blood to the lungs.

In the lungs blood picks up oxygen and drops carbon dioxide. Blood from the lungs goes to the left atrium and ventricle. The left atrium and ventricle send the blood out to the body. The left ventricle works six times harder than the right ventricle because it carries oxygenated blood.

Brain

The human brain is the central organ of the human nervous system, and with the spinal cord makes up the central nervous system. It is located in the head.

The brain consists of the cerebrum, the brainstem and the cerebellum. It controls most of the activities of the body, processing, integrating, and coordinating the information it receives from the sense organs, and making decisions as to the instructions sent to the rest of the body. The brain is contained in, and protected by, the skull bones of the head.

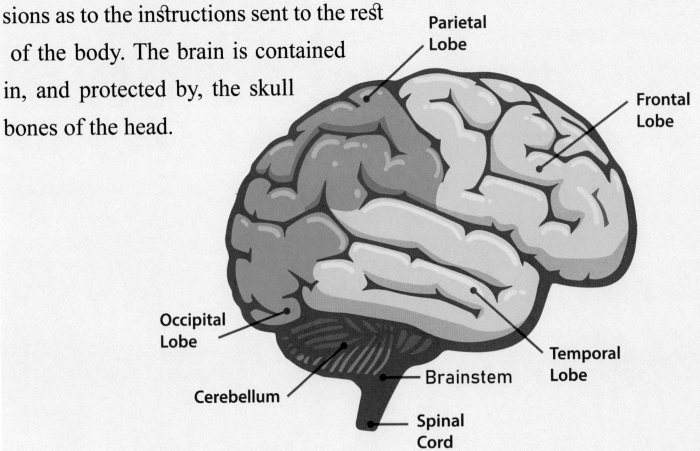

The cerebrum, the largest part of the human brain, consists of two cerebral hemispheres. Each hemisphere is conventionally divided into four lobes – the frontal, temporal, parietal, and occipital lobes.

The frontal lobe is associated with executive functions including self-control, planning, reasoning, and abstract thought, while the occipital lobe is dedicated to vision. Within each lobe, cortical areas are associated with specific functions, such as the sensory, motor and association regions. Although the left and right hemispheres are broadly similar in shape and function, some functions are associated with one side, such as language in the left and visual-spatial ability in the right.

The cerebrum is connected by the brainstem to the spinal cord.

The adult human brain weighs on average about 1.2–1.4 kg (2.6–3.1 lb) which is about 2% of the total body weight.

Higher mental functions

Eye movement

Voluntary motor function

Sensory

Somatosensory accociation

Language comprehension

Vision

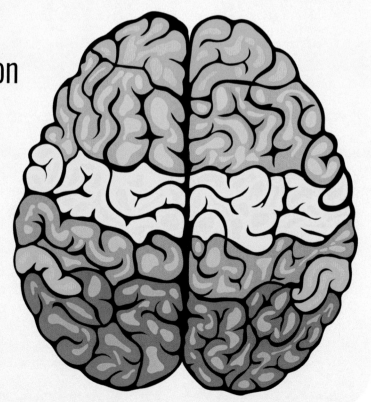

Lung

Humans have two lungs, a right lung, and a left lung. They are located in the chest on either side of the heart in the rib cage. The right lung is bigger than the left, which shares space in the chest with the heart.

Their function in the respiratory system is to extract oxygen from the air and transfer it into the bloodstream, and to release carbon dioxide from the bloodstream into the atmosphere, in a process of gas exchange.

The lungs together weigh approximately 1.3 kilograms (2.9 lb), and the right is heavier.

The tissue of the lungs can be affected by a number of respiratory diseases, including pneumonia and lung cancer.

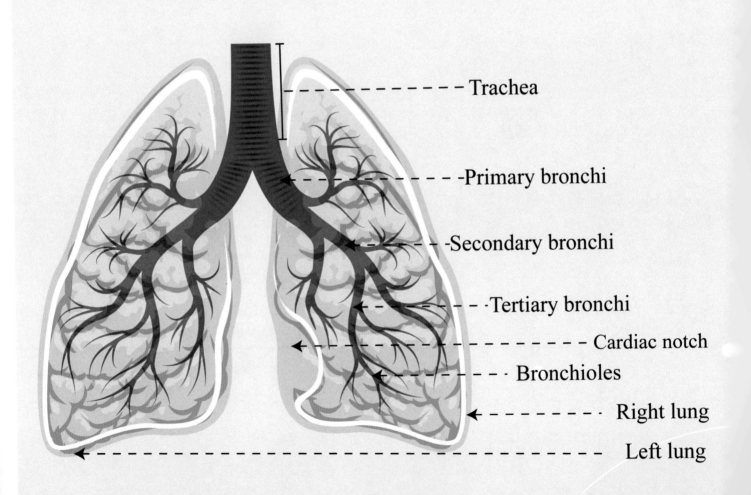

Stomach

In humans, the stomach lies between the oesophagus and the duodenum (the first part of the small intestine). It is in the left upper part of the abdominal cavity.

Like the other parts of the gastrointestinal tract, the human stomach walls consist of a mucosa, submucosa, muscularis externa, subserosa and serosa. In the human digestive system, a bolus (a small rounded mass of chewed up food) enters the stomach through the esophagus. The stomach releases proteases (protein-digesting enzymes) and hydrochloric acid, which kills or inhibits bacteria and provides the acidic pH of 2 for the proteases to work.

The body of stomach as the boluses are converted into chyme (partially digested food). Chyme slowly passes through the pyloric sphincter and into the duodenum of the small intestine, where the extraction of nutrients begins.

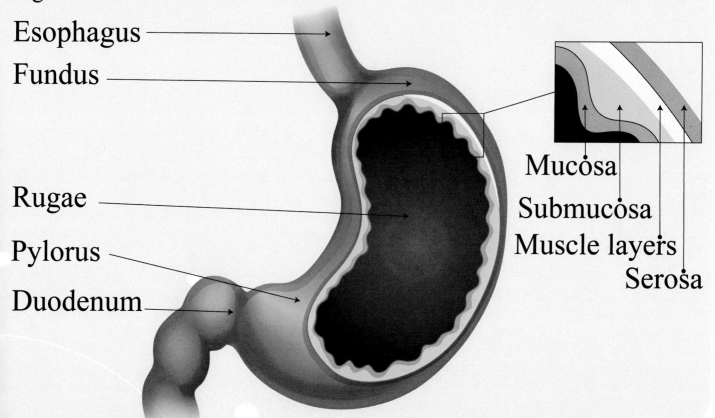

Esophagus

Fundus

Rugae

Pylorus

Duodenum

Mucosa

Submucosa

Muscle layers

Serosa

Bone

The bones are the framework of the body. Without them we would be a pile of organs on the ground and would not be able to move.

Bones also protect. The skull protects the brain and the ribs protect the heart and lungs. The jaw and cheekbones support the facial muscles, which help us eat and smile. The pelvis protects the reproductive organs, and vertebrae protect the spinal cord.

Bone tissue (osseous tissue) is a hard tissue, a type of specialized connective tissue.

In the human body at birth, there are approximately 300 bones present; many of these fuse together during development, leaving a total of 206 separate bones in the adult, not counting numerous small sesamoid bones.

There are five types of bones in the human body: long, short, flat, irregular, and sesamoid.

Long bones: most bones of the limbs, including those of the fingers and toes.
Short bones: the bones of the wrist and ankle are short bones.
Flat bones: most of the bones of the skull are flat bones.
Irregular bones: the bones of the spine, pelvis, and some bones of the skull.
Sesamoid bones: example of sesamoid bones are the patella.

The cancellous part of bones contains bone marrow. Bone marrow produces blood cells in a process called hematopoiesis. Blood cells that are created in bone marrow include red blood cells, platelets and white blood cells. Bones act as reserves of minerals important for the body, most notably calcium and phosphorus.

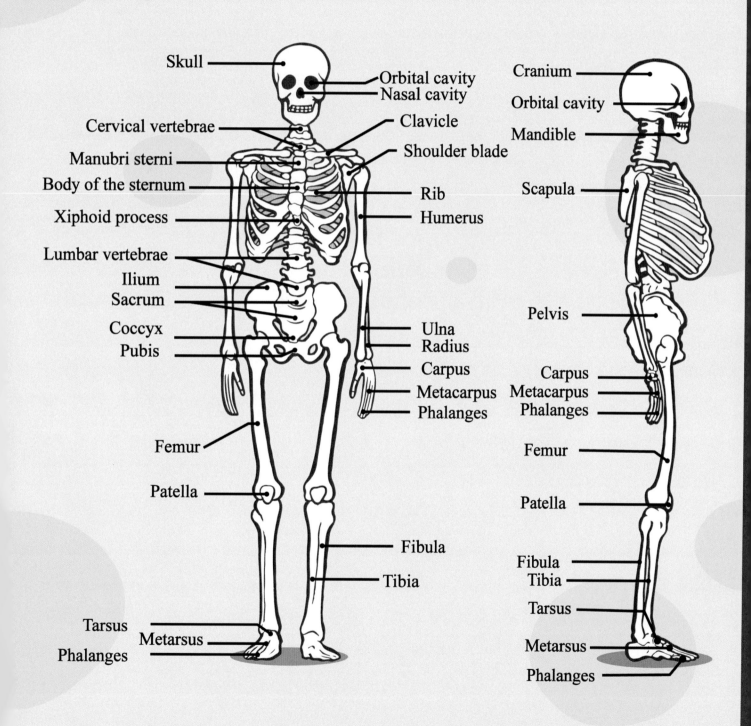

Gallbladder

is a pear-shaped organ in your abdomen. It stores about 50 ml of acidic liquid (bile) until the body needs it for digestion. That liquid helps digest fat. The gallbladder is about 7-10cm long in humans. It is dark green in color because of the bile in it. It is connected to the liver and the duodenum by the biliary tract.

Pancreas

The pancreas is an organ that makes hormones and enzymes to help digestion. The pancreas helps break down carbohydrates, fats, and proteins. The pancras is behind the stomach and is on the left side of the human body.

Liver — Stomach

Gallbladder Pancreas

Large intestine — Small intestine

Appendix

Rectum

Anus

The part of the pancreas that makes hormones is called the Islets of Langerhans. The Islets of Langerhans are a small part (2%) of the total cells in the pancreas. The Islets of Langerhans change which chemical they make depending on how much of other chemicals are already in the blood. So, the pancreas works to keep the level of chemicals in balance in the body.

(Digestion is the process of breaking down food to absorb it.)

Kidney

Kidneys are two organs in the abdomen of vertebrates that are shaped like beans. The kidney makes hormones. The two most important ones that it makes are erythropoetin and renin.

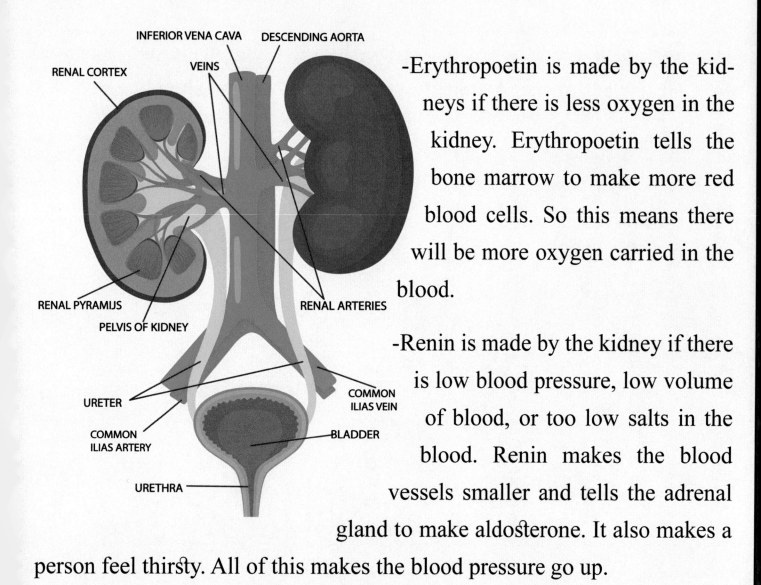

-Erythropoetin is made by the kidneys if there is less oxygen in the kidney. Erythropoetin tells the bone marrow to make more red blood cells. So this means there will be more oxygen carried in the blood.

-Renin is made by the kidney if there is low blood pressure, low volume of blood, or too low salts in the blood. Renin makes the blood vessels smaller and tells the adrenal gland to make aldosterone. It also makes a person feel thirsty. All of this makes the blood pressure go up.

The kidney's most important work is keeping homeostasis. Homeostasis means that the body keeps a stable environment inside itself. The body needs to have the consistent and proper amount of water, salt, and acid in the blood. The kidney keeps these things constant.

Liver

The liver is an organ in the abdomen. It is part of the digestive system. In humans, it is located in the right upper quadrant of the abdomen, below the diaphragm.

The liver is a reddish-brown, wedge-shaped organ with two lobes of unequal size and shape. A human liver normally weighs approximately 1.5 kg.

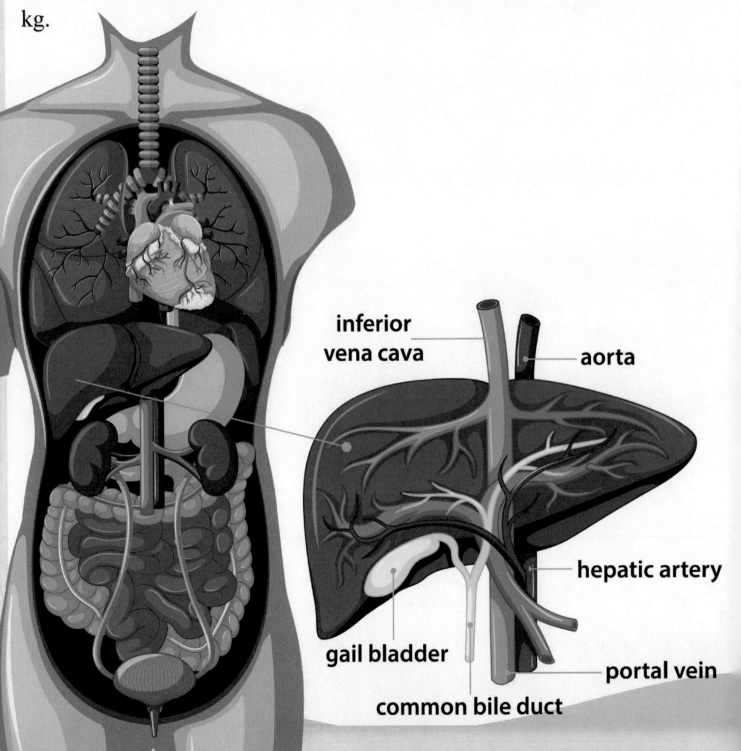

inferior vena cava

aorta

hepatic artery

gail bladder

portal vein

common bile duct

The liver is connected to two large blood vessels: the hepatic artery and the portal vein. The hepatic artery carries oxygen-rich blood from the aorta via the celiac trunk, whereas the portal vein carries blood rich in digested nutrients from the entire gastrointestinal tract and also from the spleen and pancreas.

The liver is the body's chemical factory. It does many important things:

- The liver produces (makes) bile. This is a bright yellow-green liquid that goes into the small intestines to help digest the big chunks of food we eat.
- The liver stores glucose when we eat and then puts the glucose into the blood when our blood glucose level goes down.
- The liver takes protein and fat and turns it into glucose. This is important if we have no food to eat. We can use the fat we have saved, and make it into glucose to use.
- The liver also makes some fats and cholesterol
- The liver metabolizes (breaks down) many things in the blood:
    - hemoglobin;
    - proteins like enzymes, insulin, and serum amyloid A;
    - ammonia;
    - toxins (substances that are poisons) and waste from the body.
- The liver stores (keeps) vitamins and minerals.
- The liver makes many proteins:
    - proteins that make your blood clot – called coagulation proteins
    - proteins like albumin

Intestine

The gastrointestinal tract (GI tract) is the tract from the mouth to the anus which includes all the organs of the digestive system.

The lower gastrointestinal tract includes most of the small intestine and all of the large intestine.

In humans, the small intestine is further subdivided into the duodenum, jejunum and ileum while the large intestine is subdivided into the cecum, ascending, transverse, descending and sigmoid colon, rectum, and anal canal.

The first part of the small intestine is called the duodenum, where most food is broken down by enzymes. Later, the small intestine absorbs useful compounds from the digested food.

The small intestine, usually between 6 and 7 m long. Its mucosal area in an adult human is about 30 m2 (320 sq ft).

liver — stomach — gallbladder — pancreas — duodenum — ascending colon — transverse colon — cecum — jejunum — ileum — descending colon — appendix — anal canal — sigmoid colon

The large intestine, also called the colon, absorbs water and any other nutrients, as well as vitamins made by the gut flora in the colon. Finally, waste is expelled through the anus.

The area of the large intestinal mucosa of an adult human is about 2 m2 (22 sq ft).

Skin

The human skin is the outer covering of the body, Though nearly all human skin is covered with hair, it can appear hairless. There are two general types of skin, hairy and glabrous skin (hairless).

Because it interfaces with the environment, skin plays an important immunity role in protecting the body against pathogens and excessive water loss.

Its other functions are insulation, temperature regulation, sensation, synthesis of vitamin D, and the protection of vitamin B folates. Severely damaged skin will try to heal by forming scar tissue. This is often discoloured and depigmented.

In humans, skin pigmentation varies among populations, and skin type can range from dry to non-dry and from oily to non-oily.

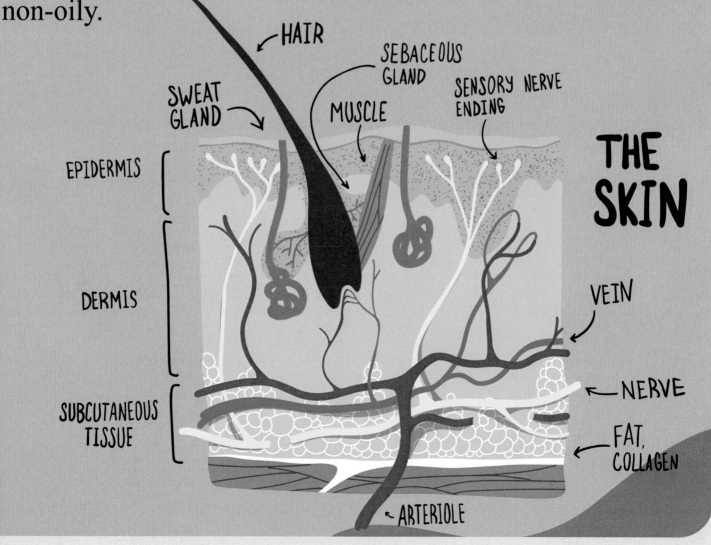

HAIR

SEBACEOUS GLAND

SENSORY NERVE ENDING

SWEAT GLAND

MUSCLE

THE SKIN

EPIDERMIS

DERMIS

VEIN

NERVE

SUBCUTANEOUS TISSUE

FAT, COLLAGEN

ARTERIOLE

Uterus

The uterus or womb is part of the reproductive system of the female body. The uterus is the place a baby grows for nine months during pregnancy. It is a pear-shaped organ inside a woman. It is behind the bladder and in front of the rectum. The uterus weighs 70 grams. The endometrium is the tissue that lines the uterus. A hormone called estrogen makes the endometrium thick with blood and fluid. This uterine lining gives the growing baby what it needs to grow. The endometrium leaves the uterus as the monthly flow of blood (menstruation). The endometrium will form again. This happens every 28 days. The number of days can be different for each women. The fertilized egg will move through the fallopian tube and into uterus. It will then attach to the endometrium.

FEMALE REPRODUCTIVE SYSTEM

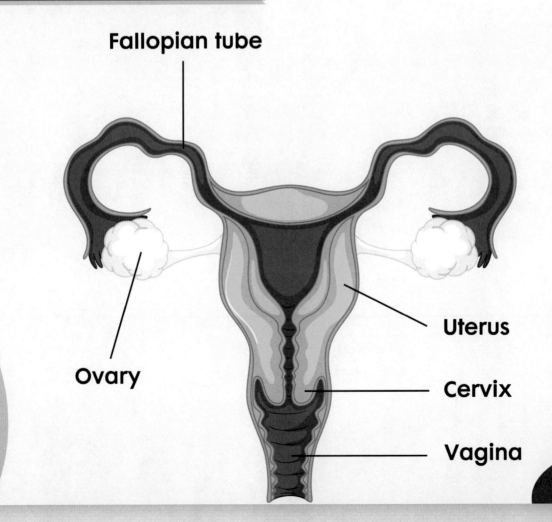

Fallopian tube

Ovary

Uterus

Cervix

Vagina

Bladder

The urinary bladder is an organ in the human body in charge of storing urine. It is the part of our urinary system. All the liquids that are drunk go through the bladder. The bladder takes in the liquid in order for the body to work. The bladder works with the kidneys. The kidneys clean the liquid we drink. This goes on util the bladder is too full to hold any more. At this point, it is roughly the size of a softball. The bladder then tells the brain that it needs to be emptied. Once this message is received to the brain, the muscles around the bladder start to squeeze and the bladder starts to contract. At the same time the bladder sends a message to the sphincters to relax and let the liquid pass.

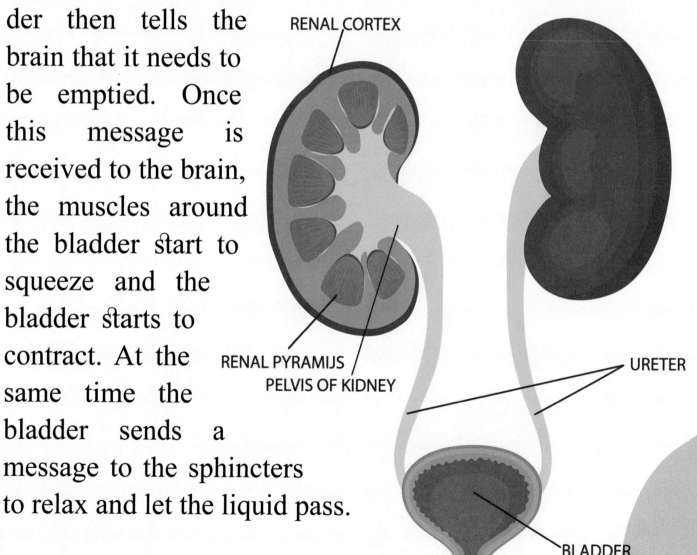

RENAL CORTEX

RENAL PYRAMIJS
PELVIS OF KIDNEY

URETER

BLADDER
URETHRA

ANATOMY OF THE URINARY SYSTEM

Systems

Systems are the most complex of the component units of the human body. A system is an organization of varying numbers and kinds of organs so arranged that together they can perform complex functions for the body.

Skeletal System:

Bones provide a rigid framework, known as the skeleton, that support and protect the soft organs of the body.

The skeleton supports the body against the pull of gravity. The large bones of the lower limbs support the trunk when standing.

The skeleton also protects the soft body parts. The fused bones of the cranium surround the brain to make it less vulnerable to injury. Vertebrae surround and protect the spinal cord and bones of the rib cage help protect the heart and lungs of the thorax.

Bones work together with muscles as simple mechanical lever systems to produce body movement.

Bones contain more calcium than any other organ.

When blood calcium levels decrease below normal, calcium is released from the bones so that there will be an adequate supply for

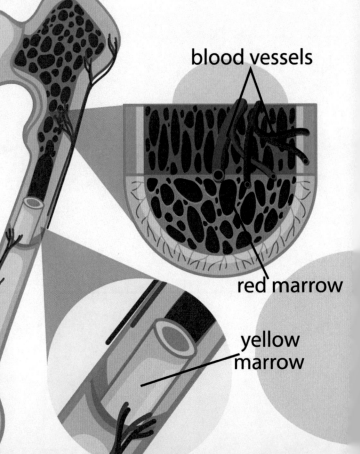

blood vessels

red marrow

yellow marrow

the needs. When blood calcium levels are increased, the excess calcium is stored in the bone matrix. The dynamic process of releasing and storing calcium goes on almost continuously. Hematopoiesis, the formation of blood cells, mostly takes place in the red marrow of the bones.

In infants, red marrow is found in the bone cavities. With age, it is largely replaced by yellow marrow for fat storage. In adults, red marrow is limited to the spongy bone in the skull, ribs, sternum, clavicles, vertebrae and pelvis. Red marrow functions in the formation of red blood cells, white blood cells and blood platelets.

Frontal
Nasal
Temporal
Orbit
Maxila
Mandible
Cervical Vertebrae
Clavicle
Sternum
Costal cartilages
Xiphoid Process
True Ribs
Humerus
False ribs
Floating rib
Lumbar vertebrae
Ilium
Radlus
Ulna
Saccrum
Coccyx
Pubis
Carpals
Metacarpals
Ischium
Phalanges
Femur
Public symphysis
Patella
Tibia
Fibula
Metatarsals
Talus
Phalanges

SKELETAL SYSTEM

Muscular System:

The muscular system is composed of specialized cells called muscle fibers. Their predominant function is contractibility. Muscles, attached to bones or internal organs and blood vessels, are responsible for movement. Nearly all movement in the body is the result of muscle contraction.

The integrated action of joints, bones, and skeletal muscles produces obvious movements such as walking and running. Skeletal muscles also produce more subtle movements that result in various facial expressions, eye movements, and respiration.

In addition to movement, muscle contraction also fulfills some other important functions in the body, such as posture, joint stability, and heat production. Posture, such as sitting and standing, is maintained as a result of muscle contraction. The skeletal muscles are continually making fine adjustments that hold the body in stationary positions.

Each skeletal muscle fiber is a single cylindrical muscle cell. An individual skeletal muscle may be made up of hundreds, or even thousands, of muscle fibers bundled together and wrapped in a connective tissue covering.

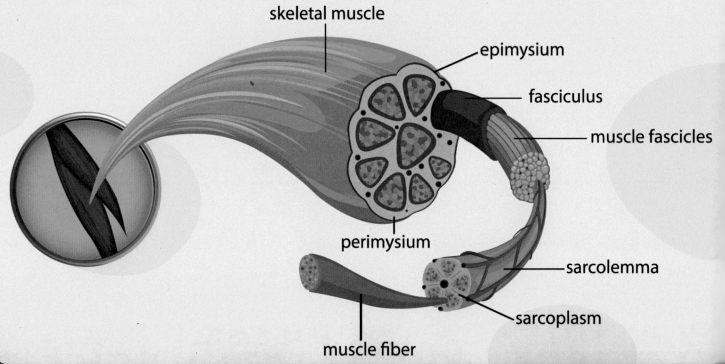

skeletal muscle

epimysium

fasciculus

muscle fascicles

perimysium

sarcolemma

sarcoplasm

muscle fiber

Muscle Types

In the body, there are three types of muscle: skeletal (striated), smooth, and cardiac.

Skeletal muscle, attached to bones, is responsible for skeletal movements.

Smooth muscle, found in the walls of the hollow internal organs such as blood vessels, the gastrointestinal tract, bladder, and uterus, is under control of the autonomic nervous system.

Cardiac muscle, found in the walls of the heart, is also under control of the autonomic nervous system.

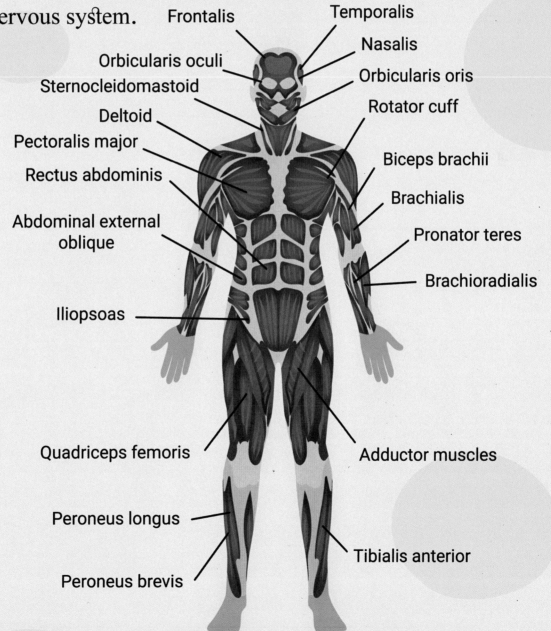

Frontalis
Temporalis
Nasalis
Orbicularis oculi
Sternocleidomastoid
Orbicularis oris
Rotator cuff
Deltoid
Pectoralis major
Biceps brachii
Rectus abdominis
Brachialis
Abdominal external oblique
Pronator teres
Brachioradialis
Iliopsoas
Quadriceps femoris
Adductor muscles
Peroneus longus
Tibialis anterior
Peroneus brevis

MUSCULAR SYSTEM

Nervous System

The nervous system is the major controlling, regulatory, and communicating system in the body. It is the center of all mental activity including thought, learning, and memory.

The nervous system is composed of organs, principally the brain, spinal cord, nerves, and ganglia. These, in turn, consist of various tissues, including nerve, blood, and connective tissue. Together these carry out the complex activities of the nervous system.

The various activities of the nervous system can be grouped together as three general, overlapping functions:

1-<u>Sensory</u>; 2-<u>Integrative</u> and 3-<u>Motor</u>.

Millions of sensory receptors detect changes, called stimuli, which occur inside and outside the body.

They monitor such things as temperature, light, and sound from the external environment.

Inside the body, the internal environment, receptors detect variations in pressure, pH, carbon dioxide concentration, and the levels of various electrolytes.

Human Nervous System

- Brain
- Cervical nerves
- Thoracic nerves
- Lumbar nerves
- Sacral nerves
- Sciatic nerve
- Spinal cord

All of this gathered information is called sensory input.

Sensory input is converted into electrical signals called nerve impulses that are transmitted to the brain.

There the signals are brought together to create sensations, to produce thoughts, or to add to memory; Decisions are made each moment based on the sensory input. This is integration.

Based on the sensory input and integration, the nervous system responds by sending signals to muscles, causing them to contract, or to glands, causing them to produce secretions. This is the motor output or motor function.

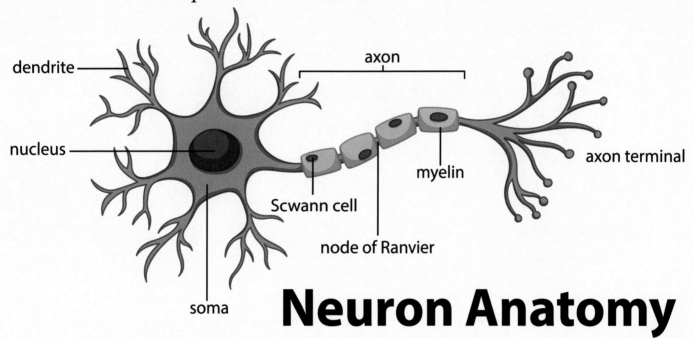

Neuron Anatomy

Nerve Tissue

Although the nervous system is very complex, there are only two main types of cells in nerve tissue. The actual nerve cell is the neuron. It is the "conducting" cell that transmits impulses and the structural unit of the nervous system. The other type of cell is neuroglia, or glial, cell. The word "neuroglia" means "nerve glue." These cells are nonconductive and provide a support system for the neurons. They are a special type of "connective tissue" for the nervous system.

Cardiovascular System

The cardiovascular system is sometimes called the blood-vascular, or simply the circulatory, system. It consists of the heart, which is a muscular pumping device, and a closed system of vessels called arteries, veins, and capillaries. As the name implies, blood contained in the circulatory system is pumped by the heart around a closed circle or circuit of vessels as it passes again and again through the various "circulations" of the body.

The heart is a muscular pump that provides the force necessary to circulate the blood to all the tissues in the body. Its function is vital because, to survive, the tissues need a continuous supply of oxygen and nutrients, and metabolic waste products have to be removed.

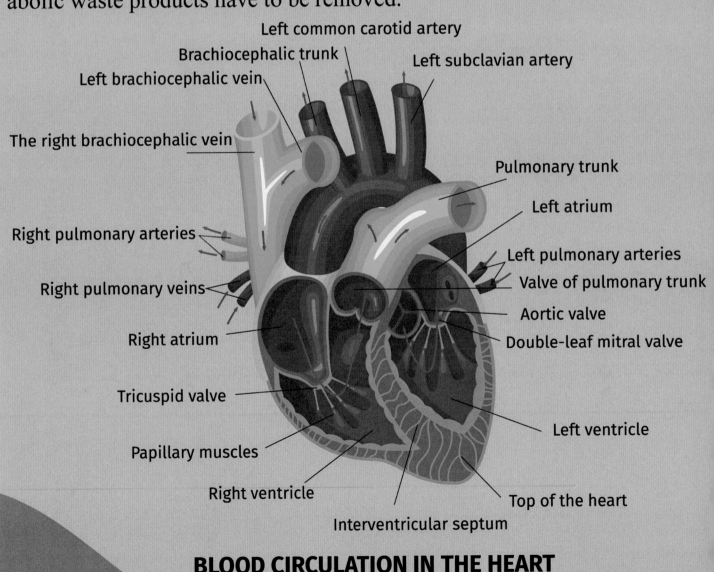

BLOOD CIRCULATION IN THE HEART

Blood flows from the right atrium to the right ventricle and then is pumped to the lungs to receive oxygen. From the lungs, the blood flows to the left atrium, then to the left ventricle. From there it is pumped to the systemic circulation.

Blood is the fluid of health, transporting disease-fighting substances to the tissue and waste to the kidneys.

Red blood cells and white blood cells are responsible for nourishing and cleansing the body. Without blood, the human body would stop working.

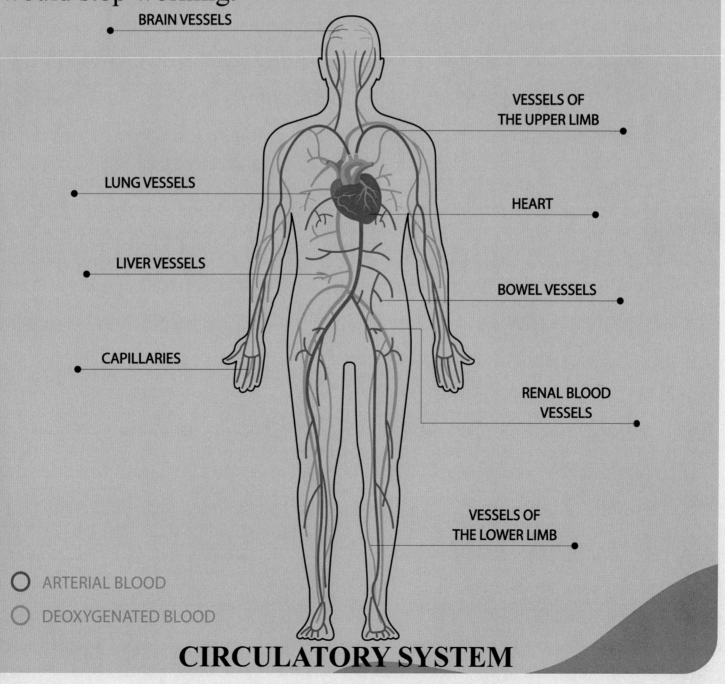

BRAIN VESSELS

VESSELS OF THE UPPER LIMB

LUNG VESSELS

HEART

LIVER VESSELS

BOWEL VESSELS

CAPILLARIES

RENAL BLOOD VESSELS

VESSELS OF THE LOWER LIMB

ARTERIAL BLOOD
DEOXYGENATED BLOOD

CIRCULATORY SYSTEM

Respiratory System:

When the respiratory system is mentioned, people generally think of breathing, but breathing is only one of the activities of the respiratory system. The body cells need a continuous supply of oxygen for the metabolic processes that are necessary to maintain life. The respiratory system works with the circulatory system to provide this oxygen and to remove the waste products of metabolism. It also helps to regulate pH of the blood.

Respiration is the sequence of events that results in the exchange of oxygen and carbon dioxide between the atmosphere and the body cells. Every 3 to 5 seconds, nerve impulses stimulate the breathing process, or ventilation, which moves air through a series of passages into and out of the lungs. After this, there is an exchange of gases between the lungs and the blood. This is called external respiration. The blood transports the gases to and from the tissue cells. The exchange of gases between the blood and tissue cells is internal respiration. Finally, the cells utilize the oxygen for their specific activities: this is called cellular metabolism, or cellular respiration. Together, these activities constitute respiration.

The respiratory conducting passages are divided into the upper respiratory tract and the lower respiratory tract. The upper respiratory tract includes the nose, pharynx, and larynx. The lower respiratory tract consists of the trachea, bronchial tree, and lungs.

HUMAN RESPIRATORY SYSTEM

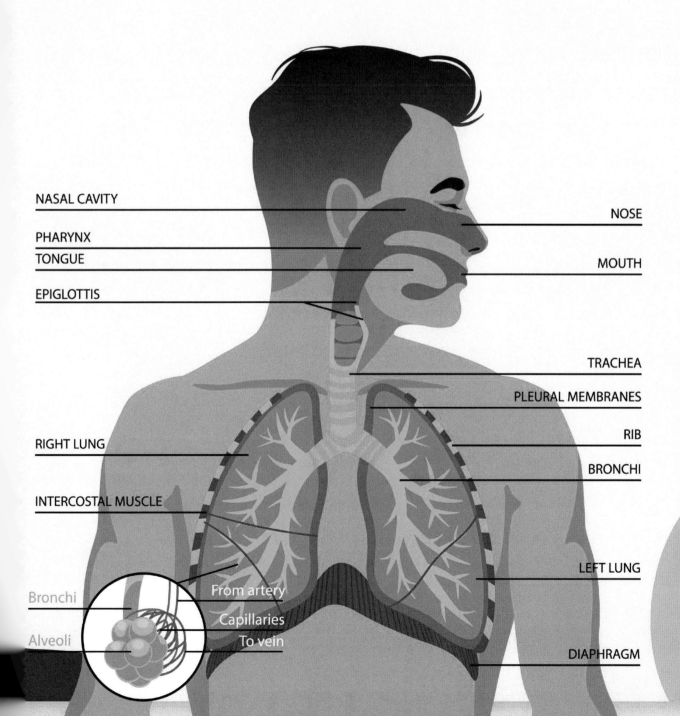

NASAL CAVITY

PHARYNX

TONGUE

EPIGLOTTIS

RIGHT LUNG

INTERCOSTAL MUSCLE

Bronchi

Alveoli

From artery

Capillaries

To vein

NOSE

MOUTH

UPPER RESPIRATORY TRACT

TRACHEA

PLEURAL MEMBRANES

RIB

BRONCHI

LEFT LUNG

DIAPHRAGM

LOWER RESPIRATORY TRACT

Digestive System:

The digestive system includes the digestive tract and its accessory organs, which process food into molecules that can be absorbed and utilized by the cells of the body. Food is broken down, bit by bit, until the molecules are small enough to be absorbed and the waste products are eliminated.

The digestive tract, also called the alimentary canal or gastrointestinal (GI) tract, consists of a long continuous tube that extends from the mouth to the anus. It includes the mouth, pharynx, esophagus, stomach, small intestine, and large intestine. The tongue and teeth are accessory structures located in the mouth. The salivary glands, liver, gallbladder, and pancreas are major accessory organs that have a role in digestion. These organs secrete fluids into the digestive tract.

Ingestion

The first activity of the digestive system is to take in food through the mouth.

Mechanical Digestion

The large pieces of food that are ingested have to be broken into smaller particles that can be acted upon by various enzymes.

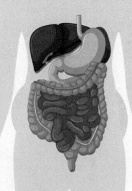

Chemical Digestion

The complex molecules of carbohydrates, proteins, and fats are transformed by chemical digestion into smaller molecules that can be absorbed and utilized by the cells.

Movements

After ingestion and mastication, the food particles move from the mouth into the pharynx, then into the esophagus.

This movement is deglutition, or swallowing. Mixing movements occur in the stomach as a result of smooth muscle contraction.

Absorption

The simple molecules that result from chemical digestion pass through cell membranes of the lining in the small intestine into the blood or lymph capillaries. This process is called absorption.

Elimination

The food molecules that cannot be digested or absorbed need to be eliminated from the body. The removal of indigestible wastes through the anus, in the form of feces, is defecation or elimination.

Regions of the digestive system can be divided into two main parts: alimentary tract and accessory organs.

The alimentary tract of the digestive system is composed of the mouth, pharynx, esophagus, stomach, small and large intestines, rectum and anus.

Associated with the alimentary tract are the following accessory organs: salivary glands, liver, gallbladder, and pancreas.

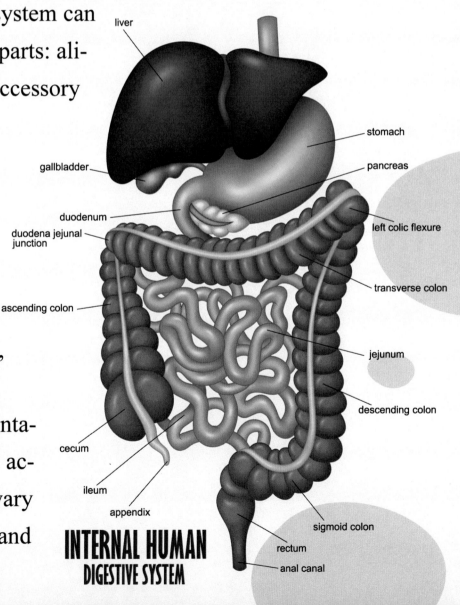

liver
stomach
pancreas
gallbladder
left colic flexure
duodenum
transverse colon
duodena jejunal junction
ascending colon
jejunum
descending colon
cecum
ileum
appendix
sigmoid colon
rectum
anal canal

INTERNAL HUMAN
DIGESTIVE SYSTEM

Reproductive System:

The major function of the reproductive system is to ensure survival of the species. Other systems in the body, such as the endocrine and urinary systems, work continuously to maintain homeostasis for survival of the individual.

Within the context of producing offspring, the reproductive system has four functions:

To produce egg and sperm cells;

To transport and sustain these cells;

To nurture the developing offspring;

To produce hormones.

The male reproductive system consists of the testes, duct system, accessory glands, and penis.

The male gonads are the testes. Their location within the scrotum is necessary for the production of viable sperm.

The female reproductive system includes the ovaries, uterine tubes, uterus, vagina, accessory glands, and external genital organs.

The female gonads are the ovaries, which are located on each side of the uterus in the pelvic cavity.

Male Reproductive System

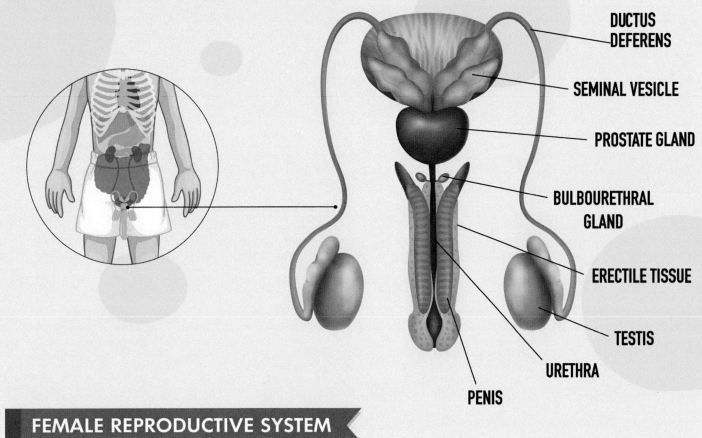

DUCTUS DEFERENS

SEMINAL VESICLE

PROSTATE GLAND

BULBOURETHRAL GLAND

ERECTILE TISSUE

TESTIS

URETHRA

PENIS

FEMALE REPRODUCTIVE SYSTEM

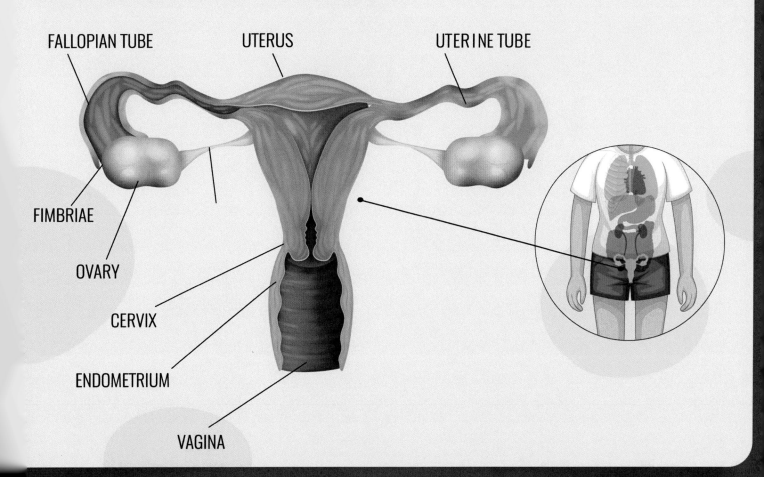

FALLOPIAN TUBE

UTERUS

UTERINE TUBE

FIMBRIAE

OVARY

CERVIX

ENDOMETRIUM

VAGINA

Urinary System:

The principal function of the urinary system is to maintain the volume and composition of body fluids within normal limits. One aspect of this function is to rid the body of waste products that accumulate as a result of cellular metabolism, and, because of this, it is sometimes referred to as the excretory system.

Although the urinary system has a major role in excretion, other organs contribute to the excretory function. The lungs in the respiratory system excrete some waste products, such as carbon dioxide and water.

The urinary system consists of the kidneys, ureters, urinary bladder, and urethra. The kidneys form the urine and account for the other functions attributed to the urinary system. The ureters carry the urine away from kidneys to the urinary bladder, which is a temporary reservoir for the urine. The urethra is a tubular structure that carries the urine from the urinary bladder to the outside.

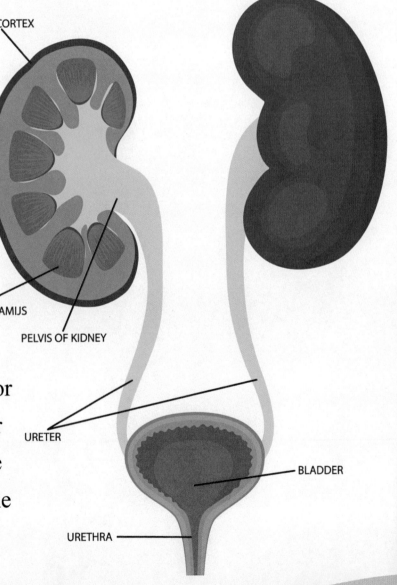

RENAL CORTEX

RENAL PYRAMIJS

PELVIS OF KIDNEY

URETER

BLADDER

URETHRA

Additional information

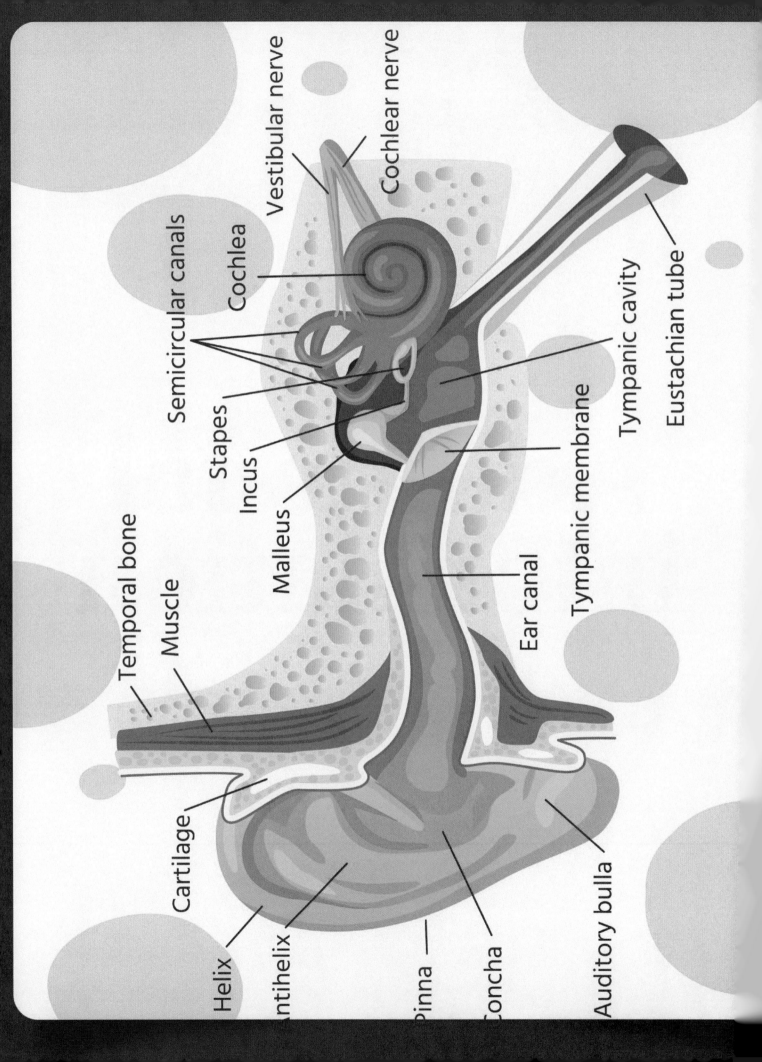

Vestibular nerve

Cochlear nerve

Semicircular canals

Cochlea

Stapes

Incus

Malleus

Temporal bone

Muscle

Tympanic cavity

Eustachian tube

Tympanic membrane

Ear canal

Cartilage

Antihelix

Helix

Pinna

Concha

Auditory bulla

EYE ANATOMY
infographics

RIGHT EYE - VIEWED FROM ABOVE

Eye lid

Lacrimal caruncle

Tear duct

Lateral rectus muscle

Choroid

Retina

Fovea centralis

Hyaloid canal

Optic nerve
Retinal blood vessels

Vitreous body

Medial rectus muscle

Sclera

Iris

Pupil

Cornea

Lens

Anterior chamber

Posterior chamber

Suspensory ligaments

Ciliary body and muscle

LUNGS
Danger of smoking

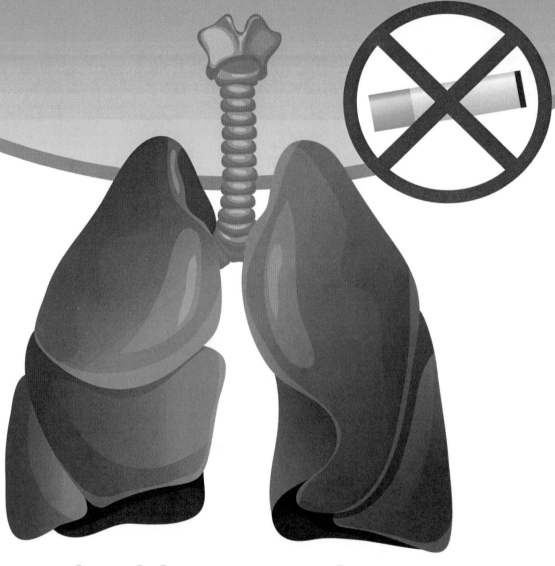

healthy lungs   smoker lungs

The vast majority (85%) of cases of lung cancer are due to long-term tobacco smoking.

The major method of prevention is the avoidance of risk factors, including smoking and air pollution.

STOMACH
GASTRITIS

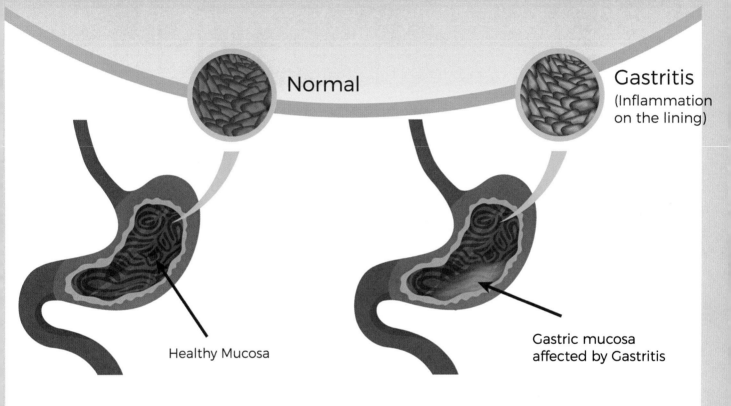

Normal

Gastritis
(Inflammation on the lining)

Healthy Mucosa

Gastric mucosa
affected by Gastritis

Healthy
Stomach

Gastric mucosa
affected by Gastritis

Junk food is unhealthy food that is high in calories from sugar or fat, with little dietary fiber, protein, vitamins, minerals, or other important forms of nutritional value.

Gastritis is inflammation of the lining of the stomach. It may occur as a short episode or may be of a long duration. Gastritis is believed to affect about half of people worldwide.

Pregnant Fetus Anatomy

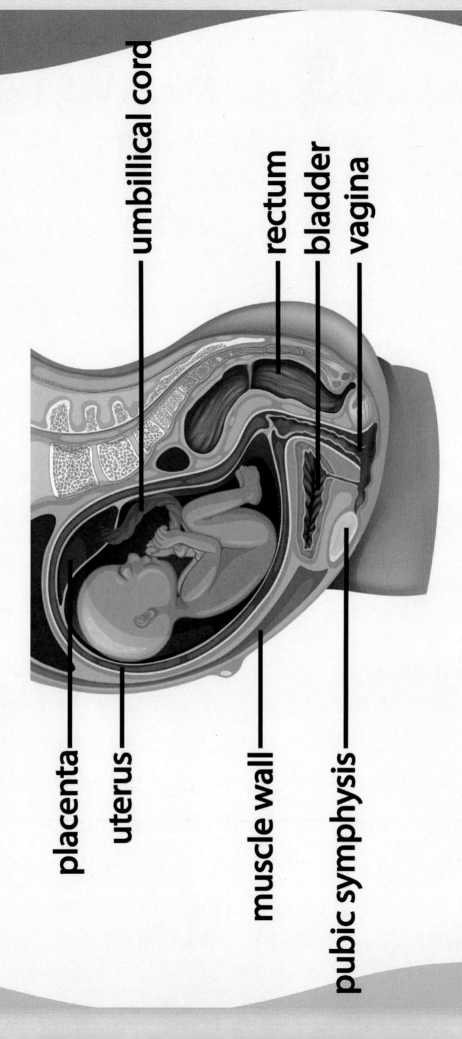

umbillical cord

rectum

bladder

vagina

placenta

uterus

muscle wall

pubic symphysis

Made in the USA
Middletown, DE
02 September 2024

60311704R00024